Family Promises

Other Books by Laura Boss

Stripping, Chantry Press, 1982

On the Edge of the Hudson, Cross-Cultural Communications, 1986

Stripping Sulla Sponda Dell' Hudson, Cross-Cultural Communications and Coop. Editrice Antigruppo Sicilano, English-Italian, 1987 American Literary Translator Association Award (translated by Nat and Nina Scammacca)

On the Edge of the Hudson (English-Macedonian), HK and Cross-Cultural Communications, 1989 (translated by Jozo Boskovski)

Reports from the Front, Cross-Cultural Communications, 1995

Arms: New and Selected Poems, Guernica Editions, 1999

Flashlight, Guernica Editions, 2010

The Best Lover, NYQ Books, 2017

As Editor:

Time Is a Toy: The Selected Poems of Michael Benedikt, edited by John Gallaher and Laura Boss, University of Akron, 2014

Family Promises

Poems by

Laura Boss

The New York Quarterly Foundation, Inc.
New York, New York

NYQ Books™ is an imprint of The New York Quarterly Foundation, Inc.

The New York Quarterly Foundation, Inc.
P. O. Box 470
Beacon, NY 12508

www.nyq.org

First Edition

Set in New Baskerville

Layout and Design by Raymond P. Hammond

Cover Painting: "Engagement", 19" x 25", watercolor and gouache on paper
by Linda Hillringhouse | lindahillringhouse.zenfolio.com

Author Photograph by Amanda Rose Boss

Library of Congress Control Number: 2021937667

ISBN: 978-1-63045-090-8

Family Promises

Acknowledgments

"What I Knew About My Father," "At Her Other Grandmother's Funeral," "This is the Year of Medical Appointments," "Almost Addicted to Facebook," "So Much Time Has Gone By Since I've Heard from Him," "My Two Lives," "Hospital Bed," "Unconditional Love," "Obsession," "Whenever I See a Man," "A Good Morning BLue Sky," and "As Winter Sets In" all appeared previously in a special tribute section to Laura Boss in the *Paterson Literary Review #49.*

"On Hearing of John Ashbery's Death" first appeared in *Exit 13.*

Contents

For my family who has always
tried to keep their promises
and for my son Barry who has always kept his.

FAMILY PROMISES

When I was sixteen,
my mother made me promise
not to tell my father
he was dying of pancreatic cancer.
She made me promise
not to tell my thirteen year old brother.
She asked me to care for my father
while she was teaching since
I was home by 12:30 from
my double session high school
while she didn't get home
from Public School 11 until after four.
My father had a naturally sweet disposition
and I learned how pain could change even
the sunniest of natures.
I learned to lie that fall
I lied to my father who wanted to believe
he'd recover from painful "pancreatitis."
I lied to my brother.
I learned to lie by omission.
I smiled and lied to
my best friend, my teachers,
my friends on the school paper
when they asked me if I were all right.
I even lied to my mother and told
her I was not depressed as
she managed to teach and do lesson
plans and spend nights with my
father as the tiny black and white tv droned
on—mostly Yankee games that he couldn't
focus on as we all waited for the nurse who
lived next door to arrive with the morphine shot
prescribed by her husband, a resident at
Memorial Hospital in Manhattan.
After my father died,
my mother spiraled into depression

though she continued to teach.
My brother turned atheist.
I learned to keep smiling
and lying and for years saying I was fine
no matter what random disaster
plummeted toward me
and those I loved.

HOW OUR CHILDREN LIVE

—written the day after the terrorist attack near
Stuyvesant High School, October 2017

Years ago, the week after 9/11, my six year old granddaughter
sits in her suburban first grade class as the principal phones
her home to say Amanda's desk mate's father
(a soccer coach for his son's team) is still "missing"
That father will never coach another soccer team again
And each year my granddaughter (and all of us)
listens for his name read
on tv at the 9/11 Memorial
After her parents split, my granddaughter at eight
moves with her mother and younger sister to
live with her other grandmother, her "abuela,"
in an immaculate apartment on a sometimes
drive-by-shooting street in Washington Heights
My granddaughter tells me not to point at anyone
when I pick her up in my car for a rare jaunt to the Met
"He could be a gang member, have a gun,
and think you're pointing at him"

In eighth grade my granddaughter is thrilled
to be accepted at Stuyvesant High School not only
because it is such a top public high school but also
because it has a swimming pool though
like many teen age girls, she eventually decides to
forego swimming in favor of her hair not looking tangled
and water logged each day
and instead becomes active in Aspira and involved
with social justice in the Hispanic school community and beyond

At graduation, my granddaughter wins the poetry prize
at Stuyvesant but decides to be a computer science major
at Harvard where she has won a full scholarship
I see her trying to have a life without the struggles of a
free-lance poet like me or her separated parents who have each
fallen into unexpected unemployment disaster
as Amanda continues to tutor kids for free in the inner city

Last May, my granddaughter's graduation from Harvard
    is a day that goes into our memory scrapbooks
    —hers, of course, her mother's, her abuela's, and mine—

I wish her father, my son, could also be here
    but I try not to focus on his absence
My granddaughter introduces us to her new
    and possibly first boyfriend
He brings her flowers and seems slightly nervous
    meeting her family for the first time—
My granddaughter has warned me not to ask him any questions
    and whether it is because he is Vietnamese and
    she's afraid I'll embarrass her by asking anything personal
    —or even worse, possibly politically incorrect
I think she has probably said this to all of her family here today
But I like him immediately because he arrives with a bouquet of
    tiger lilies for her and he's summa cum laude
    from a nearby fine college
    and though I don't know anything about him
    summa cum laude tells me he's not just bright
    but also conscientious
When she started college, I told Amanda no one
    escapes without getting heartbroken
    but I know like so many other random things,
    love is one more thing I have no control over
    though I send a message to the gods of love to keep
    my granddaughter safe from the end of love
    with all its emotional hell
My granddaughter has signed a contract
    to work in the internet field
She will move to San Francisco
    and though I will miss her, her future seems secure
    unless some random plane crash, earthquake, flood,
    disease, accident finds her
And I know there is obviously no guaranteed safety in our world

Today I read where the terrorist, a father of three children,
rammed his rental Home Depot Truck
into a Stuyvesant school bus
near the school and into the same running path
my granddaughter once ran with her classmates
rammed his rental Home Depot truck
into that school bus where two students were hurt,
where eight cyclists died, fifteen wounded,
chaos, where some students looked out upper floor windows
and took photos with their cell phones,
seeing kids running to safety, mothers
and nannies running with strollers
seeing crushed bikes, spokes dented and bloody
the worst terror attack in the City since 9/11

And I think how random terrorism
or just violence is something our children
always live with though try not to focus on—
how by just minutes or even years
we are lucky or unlucky—
that it could have been us, our children
grandchildren on that bus or pathway at
that moment as a truck hurtled towards us

Still, I think our children will continue to have
the sweet toughness and resilience of one
of the injured students on that Stuyvesant school bus
yesterday who despite his wounds returns to
his classes at Stuyvesant today trying not to let the attack
ruin his record, still trying for 100% attendance

Yes, this is how our children live; this is how we all now live

WE BROKE UP OVER DRUGS (1983)

—for Gregory Corso

We broke up over drugs
  Your decades old heroin addiction—
  my puritanical response to your shooting up
We broke up over drugs
  Driving through the Lincoln Tunnel
  each morning so you could buy heroin
  labeled "poison" in glassine envelopes
  near Chrystie Street and not being able
  to wait until we got home to shoot up immediately
My worrying the police would stop you
  And arrest you at the small park
  or arrest me on the way back
  to my apartment and find the heroin
  and "the works"—the clean needles
  you also bought that day
We broke up over drugs
  Your selling a page from your notebook
  or a sketch with a new poem
  to Andreas Brown at Gotham Book Mart
  on West 47th Street so you'd have money
  for tomorrow's drugs
We broke up over drugs
  My worrying I'd get Aids from you
  though you said you only used
  clean needles and mostly you slept
  on my brown velvet sofa
  watching a baseball game
  if you weren't nodding off
  though sometimes you wrote
  in your Chinese red silk notebook
  with your Mont Blanc pen
  you asked me to buy for you
  and to buy one for myself
  though I never did

We broke up over drugs
  Your promising to get clean
  and go to the methadone clinic
  and my finding out you had
  gone only once
We broke up over drugs
  Your loving your drugs more than me
  Your abandonment of your kids—
  each one with a different mother
My trying to keep your 8 year old son Max
  From San Francisco who was spending
  a week with us supplied with toys,
  Radio Shack stuff while you
  dozed on the sofa

I remember your saying
  "If Max ever does drugs,
  I'll kill myself"
Not realizing (or maybe you did)
  You were killing yourself every day

A GUCCI SUITCASE FILLED WITH HEROIN

—for G.C.

Years ago in the lobby of an Atlantic City hotel, I clutched a Gucci suitcase
filled with enough heroin to wean Gregory slowly off it.
The idea for him to get off it was mine.
The idea for it to happen in Atlantic City was his.
And he told me it was too dangerous for him with his beatnik look to carry
the suitcase.
And according to him, I looked so innocent and proper no one would
question me.
I worried about being arrested.

But I was obsessed with him and getting him off drugs
more than I worried about what trouble I could be in.
His love of gambling was almost as strong as his love of drugs
and I was beginning to finally realize much more than his love of me.
I thought each day I would give him fewer of the glassine envelopes
labeled "Poison" until he was finally free of his decades long habit.

But, of course, I was wrong,
wrong to trust him not to sneak more,
wrong to trust him not to go through all the gambling money,
wrong to trust myself and
my belief that my love would be strong enough to
change what no other woman before me had been able to change.

Later that night, after he had pawned
the watch I had given him,
we headed back to my apartment above the Hudson River
with its spectacular view of the New York skyline
where we had been living with his unfinished paintings on the walls—
we fought—I raged about his breaking his promise;
he raged about my rage.

He threw some of his poems down my incinerator
probably knowing how that would also shock me after
I thought nothing else he could do would.
He called his old girlfriend who unlike me didn't mind
his drugging as much as she did his drinking as she
had once told me—

He called a taxi and left for her place.
He was often called "l'Enfant Terrible" of poetry in literary essays.
But I thought of myself that night as a woman wild enough or,
more accurately, stupid enough to do anything for a man she loved—
even if it meant her own possible destruction.

HOW MY PARENTS MET

My parents met in a Chinese
nightclub Chin Lee's close to Radio
City where my mother worked as
a bookkeeper and my father was
their part time accountant—
though not a CPA

My mother had a steady boyfriend
Max who was a doctor and
someone my grandmother
approved of in those Depression
years when money was more
than tight—and security was
spelled with a capital S

My mother had graduated from
Normal School—the first of
her family to go to college
but hadn't been able to
secure a job as a teacher yet

She said my father was "fresh"
that he had put his hand
on her knee under the table
where they were working

But I think she must have liked it
because that doctor was out of
her life soon after—
though my grandmother had
told my father when he
appeared at
my grandparents' railroad
apartment over their five
small stores near Sheepshead

Bay on a night the doctor was
visiting my mother to "tell
the doctor you're her cousin"
But my father didn't
The men played gin rummy
My father with his photographic
memory won the game,
won my mother

And sometimes I wonder
if something runs in my DNA
on the maternal side
when we women don't listen
to our mothers
but make the choice
of a man based on
how we feel when
his hand touches our knee
under the table

WHAT I KNEW ABOUT MY FATHER

What I didn't know about my father
was my fault for not asking questions
for not knowing enough to ask questions
I knew his sunny disposition
I knew he could memorize the Odd Fellow
Inauguration book when he was Grand Master
I knew he could add four columns of figures in
his head
I knew he worked for the Atomic Energy Commission
and before that the OPA and OPS and
before that the Manhattan Project in Tennessee
and did something
involving numbers not science

I knew when he was often traveling home,
he would bring me a box of marzipan fruit:
strawberries, bananas, cherries because he knew
I loved that candy
I knew he insisted my mother sleep late on Sunday
mornings when he was home and made my
younger brother and me his original chocolate
French toast for breakfast

I knew he had been married when he was 18 because he
got a "nice" Jewish girl pregnant and later she miscarried
and this was years before he married my mother
I knew he had thought he would never have
a child and it would be the end of his family line
since his two older sisters had never married and were
too old to have children
I knew he had never been Bar Mitzvahed because his father
was an atheist
I knew his parents had been divorced and remarried
and divorced again and his father remarried someone else

I knew money was always a problem for my father growing up
and that he had delivered milk at 5am from his mother's
grocery before he left for school

I knew he never had a mark lower than an A on his report cards
since my mother looked up his records when she was
subbing in an old school in the city he'd attended

I knew he never made enough money to satisfy my mother
though he always worked and worked
I knew he didn't deserve the pain (who does) from pancreatic
cancer when I was 16 and my brother 13

I knew I was his favorite

THIS THANKSGIVING

This Thanksgiving my husband and I went to Atlanta
    to spend Thursday through Sunday
    with his very caring daughter
Jim and I had gotten up at 3:20 a.m. and were
    at the airport by 5
My new husband (not so different
    from my other husband so many decades ago)
    likes to be prompt so being really early
    is not a problem for me
My husband had a free companion ticket for me
    and things were good on the plane
At the airport my husband stopped to buy
    his usual lottery ticket
    while his daughter patiently waited
When we got to her house, the turkey was
    still baking
Her son, her husband, and my husband watched
    one of the football games on tv
When dinner was ready, I mentioned an old tradition
    from my family from years ago of going around the table
    and everyone saying something
    each one was grateful for
Instead they said grace and crossed themselves and
    said they were grateful for the food
I said Amen with them
I didn't cross myself since
    I'm Jewish and my husband who converted
    to Judaism when he married his second wife
    didn't cross himself either

I thought how my son's children were spending
    Thanksgiving with their mother and abuela
    whom they had lived with since their parents
    split when they were in kindergarten and
    third grade

I thought of my older son and his children who
    spend every Thanksgiving with their
    other grandmother, my daughter-in-law's mother
I thought about my younger son alone on Thanksgiving
    and wondered if any of my grandchildren would phone or
    email me today unlike last Thanksgiving

During dinner, we said how delicious the sausage
    stuffing was that my step daughter's husband had made
    from a family recipe
We spoke of how good the squash soufflé was that my
    stepdaughter had made
We commented on how much their fourteen-year-old son
    had grown since our last visit

I thought how happy my husband seemed to be with his
    daughter and her family
And I thought to myself I should be grateful for this and
    that my own grandchildren are having a traditional
    Thanksgiving with at least one of their grandparents
And I love my grandchildren so much that just knowing they
    are happy is more than enough

WHERE I GO FROM HERE

Where I go from here
is not going to be too far
since I just celebrated a
birthday whose number says almost over

Where I go from here is maybe backward
trying to find old friends who have disappeared,
old third cousins, old classmates
who in my forward moving years
years ago (and probably theirs too) lost touch
I wonder if they're ok, if they're still alive

It's odd this having fewer years ahead
where once the future spread
out like a long glowing road with
no near end—
Where once there were so many divergent paths
with no near end—
Where once there were so many divergent paths
I could have taken and sometimes did
Where once I stopped for years
and focused on my kids—their future lives
where they were going

I guess I'll just try to call some old friends—
but with cell phones, no directory listings for
them anymore—

I'll hope their minds are still alert—
that they have avoided the Alzheimer's epidemic
in our age group—
That they might say—I was thinking about you too

And maybe sooner not later, I'll pack up my journals
so my grown kids and grandchildren so busy
(and I'm glad they are) with their own lives
might one day after I'm gone
pick up one of these journals
and discover who their mother or grandmother really was

OVERNIGHT HIKE

When I think of hiking,
I remember Camp Madeline Mulford
Girl Scout Camp when I was 11
It was a big deal our overnight hike—
something different from our
open canvas tents
where we slept with mesquite netting
covering our faces,
the scent of citronella,
the scary night walks
up to the outhouses
on a nearby hill

The major event of our summer
was this hike to a grassy area
(although it all looked
the same to me used to tiny
houses with alleys between
them and a patch of back yard)

We placed our coarse blankets on the
grass before twilight
and I noticed cows munching
grass nearby

I couldn't sleep and spent the night
holding my flashlight
and writing a long poem
in my notebook (originally given
to me with instructions to "write a letter home
each day" which I didn't and where
my dislike of writing letters probably
started)

And somehow I remember sleeping under the stars
for the first time, the cows in the nearby

meadow, the vastness of our universe,
the insignificance of myself in it,
recognizing the infinite wonder and beauty of
our world for the first time

In the morning we began the hike up
some mountain with a Native
American name (although
we called it Indian in
politically incorrect and unaware
1949) but a name that
today eludes me

I was not even half way up the mountain
when I realized I didn't
have the energy to go
even one more step

My counselors who seemed much older to me
but were probably 19 and 20
ordered two other girls
to grab my feet and shoulders
and carry me up this
"Girl Scout Mt. Everest"

My tent mates were not happy
but like good Girl Scouts
they followed orders

On Visiting Day two weeks later
the entire camp put on a show:
my prose poem produced
like an amateur skit that involved
the boring cows I had written
about but left out the wonder
of our place in our vast
planet under the distant stars

The poem-play was as well received as anything
    produced by kids is received
    by their parents (those
    campers playing cows got
    the most applause)

That summer was the last hike I ever took

But it was not the last poem I would ever write

AT HER OTHER GRANDMOTHER'S FUNERAL

—for Bianca

When I see my granddaughter with her
hands covering her eyes and face,
I realize she is quietly crying—
so no one will notice her tears—
so no one will notice her soft sobs
her hands try to muffle
Earlier, she sat next to me so I wouldn't
be completely alone during this wake
for her other grandmother, her abuela Judith
she had lived with since kindergarten
when her mother and my son had split
In all the years and all the time we have spent together
(though never as many as I would have liked),
I have never seen her cry(at least since she was
a toddler)
I instinctively put my arm around her shoulder,
knowing it really won't take away grief—just
perhaps give a bit of comfort, maybe not, maybe yes
She doesn't pull away—
Still, after a while my college granddaughter excuses herself
to greet one of her former teachers from public school
who has worked with her other grandmother
She excuses herself again once she is back to say
"I need to check on my mom" who is sitting
in the front row
I watch as Bianca wobbles slightly on her new black
heels, new black mourning dress (so different
from her usual uniform of sneakers, jeans, and hoodies)
There are about 300 people in this chapel, some drifting
in and out, some leaving, new ones appearing
during this six hour wake that apparently is the actual funeral
service, eulogies by my granddaughter's mother in Spanish
(out of respect for her mother's friends and family)
though she herself speaks elegant English normally;
a eulogy by the sister of abuela who has flown in from Puerta Rico;
a choir from abuela's church, another eulogy in Spanish
from the pastor of her Baptist Church

I'm surprised by the crowd though Judith has lived in her
Washington Heights apartment for 50 years
when she and her husband settled here
And maybe there are this many people at her wake maybe
because she has been so active
working at the voting booths in the basement,
maybe because she greeted new arrivals in her high-rise;
maybe because she was active in local politics,
maybe because she has worked at a neighborhood school
as a teaching assistant for so many years though
once when young she had been a teacher in Puerta Rico;
maybe because she has been active in her church

Her potato salad is legendary in her family as are her empanadas

She seems to have liked everyone
except my son whom she hated
I don't think she really liked me because I was his mother
but she was smart enough not to say
anything to my face about me,
just my son on the rare occasions we saw each other—
my older granddaughter's graduation from Harvard,
this younger granddaughter's high school graduation from Brooklyn Tech

And I wonder, am I any different from any
other parent or grandparent I know
When our children or grandchildren hurt,
we would do anything to eliminate their sadness,
would take it on ourselves if we could,
wrap their sorrows around us like lycra if it were only possible
even though we realize we have no way to make their heartbreak disappear

And I think what a good grandmother my granddaughter's other grandmother
must have been to drown Bianca in such sorrow

FOUND CAT

The coldest day in February
I hear a mewing on our shared walkway
A cat leaps up the steps still mewing
and rubs its body against my legs

Black, blackest with startling green
eyes and bones sticking out of its
famished body

I am not a "cat person"
I am a "dog person"
I am allergic to cats which
may be why I'm a "dog person"

Still, I give the cat some of my dog's food outside
My husband tells me this is a mistake
that I'll never get rid of the cat
The cat sleeps on our doormat
Again, I feed it outside
The next day I bring it inside
worried about ringworm it might have because
of a bare circle around its tail

But I'm more worried the cat will freeze or starve to death
I call the police in three neighboring towns
but no one has reported a lost pet
I put up signs Found Cat and my phone number
in my neighborhood
No one calls

This affectionate cat is obviously
an abandoned cat
I buy a litter box it immediately uses
I get advice from a friend who
used to rescue cats before she got sick
I take the cat to our dog's vet

She does not have ringworm but gets tested for other diseases
I get her rabies shots and all the other necessary shots and vaccines

I find out she is a he
and a year and a half old
with no identity chip
The vet says he's very friendly
and sweet (which I know)
The vet tells me the cat is extremely underweight
He does not have ringworm
He is not cat HIV positive

After the test results, they phone
and tell me he has an infectious disease
and needs medication for three weeks to clear it up
and I need to give that medicine
to my fourteen year old Bichon as well

I worry the cat will scratch
our dog's spindle tumor
and have covers put on the cat's claws
I've called Saint Hubert's
but they say they're full
and aren't taking cats now
I call two animal control places
but they can't promise me
the cat won't be euthanized
I feed the cat baby food chicken
and baby rice cereal for his diarrhea

The cat sleeps on my placemat
on the dining room table.
He loves me to pet him
under his chin and behind his ears.
He is ravenous and constantly mews for food
and jumps on the kitchen counter

if I go into the kitchen to try to prepare even breakfast
My husband, Bichon Nelly and I lock ourselves
in the bedroom at night
because of my cat allergies
The cat roams the rest of the apartment

I feed Nelly on the bed
so the cat won't eat her food.
At night the cat sometimes runs
down to the basement
where I keep his food and litter box

He runs up and sleeps on my placemat
or outside our closed bedroom door
or just roams the tiny apartment
while we stay locked in our bedroom

In the middle of the night the cat starts mewing
and doesn't stop until I come out
take him on my lap and pet him
he mews and I give him more food—
The cortisone shot in my knee is wearing off
and I'm having trouble
bringing his food to the basement
as well as cleaning his litter box three times a day

The cat is now on cat food and I take him back
to the vet once he's off the medicine for three weeks

The cat in four weeks has gone
from 5 pounds 1 ounce to 9 pounds 6 ounces
He is no longer underweight

The cat is ready to be neutered
I have spent my monthly freelance
earnings on this cat
No one seems to want him at this moment
though I notice my husband seems fonder of him each day
as do I through my sneezes and itchy face

THIS IS THE YEAR OF MEDICAL APPOINTMENTS

When I ask my cousin who has retired to Florida
how she and her husband (my blood cousin)
spend their time, she answers,
"We spend our time going to
medical appointments"

And so it seems for my husband and me
and most of our friends our age

My husband's EKGs and
hospital tests to see
if he is ready for
the heart valve
since the orthopedist won't
do surgery for
the knee replacement
my husband needs until
after he has the valve done

Meanwhile, the gastroenterologist at his office
recommends a colonoscopy
though he also warns of its risks
at my husband's age

And the podiatrist wants to see
me every two weeks until
my foot problem improves
(I am sick of his golf and sports
and People outdated magazines
and wish he'd subscribe to Vanity Fair)

The ophthalmologist tells me I will
need cataract surgery in
the near future as
my husband recently had

The orthopedist gives me a shot
of cortisone for my knee and asks
if I have time to go to rehab
three times a week to
strengthen my leg muscles

She tells me after she looks at
X-rays last month that
I have torn rotator cuffs
in both shoulders and to
stop carrying a heavy shoulder
bag and to stop carting my
book bag filled with books
I need for workshops

I tell her I enjoy the magazines in her waiting
room (where my husband and I
spend so many hours)

My primary physician at my physical tells
me I need to schedule appointments:
for a bone scan
for a mammogram
for the dermatologist
for the hematologist

And my husband reminds me we have
an appointment tomorrow at the vet's
to see if the abandoned cat we recently
brought inside is free of his infection

Maybe, I'll just forget my appointments and take care of the cat

AT MY AGE

At my age I only compare myself in looks to women
around my age—
I've found it's the only way to stay sane
Most of the women of my generation in their
late 60's or 70's are grateful not to be struggling
with arthritic knees, bad backs,
maybe even chemo

But still I admit at times to fleetingly
think about how I look though I wish this were not true—
(and have a feeling I'm not the only one)
I finally know to never compare myself to a
twenty year old student in my creative writing class—
Even the plain ones with their thick dewey skin are beautiful
And I never ever compare myself to 40-year-old's
like Angelina Jolie, Halle Berry or Jennifer Anniston

But, still, I do measure myself against the glamorous icons (and
so happy they exist) of my age group: Jane Fonda, Dianna Ross,
Blondie, Raquel Welch
though knowing even these goddesses could at their age
break a hip
have a stroke
have a bad mammogram

But, suddenly, I remind myself of one beautiful woman who
just turned 75 and will not lose her physical strength or looks to
age, a woman you will never see with a cane or jowls.

Of course, it's Wonder Woman
eternally beautiful
unless her male creator suddenly decides
to cause her demise
by just putting down his pen forever

ALMOST ADDICTED TO FACEBOOK

I have three close friends
And I have 450 Facebook Friends
I know about 30 of them
    (most through poetry readings)

I have no idea who 300 of
    my Facebook Friends are
    but we seem to have some
    link through poetry
I use Facebook the way I used
    to use the post office years
    ago sending out fliers and
    publicity on new books and readings
And I must admit Facebook saves me
    lots of money on postage

Many of my Facebook Friends also
    do this and I appreciate the
    practicality of this
But many of my Facebook Friends
    seem to use Facebook for
    social chatter and connection
    to hundreds that they really
    don't know with announcements :
    that they have a bad cold
    they are going to the dentist
    they are currently eating incredible
    rigatoni Bolognaise
    at a Manhattan restaurant
    or today would have been
    their parents' 70th wedding
    anniversary and they
    post a vintage photo of their
    parents
    or a photo of their kids in
    their Easter outfits
    or the birthday of Emily Dickinson
    along with one of
    her legendary poems

And, of course, every day Facebook
    notifies me it's at least one of my
    Facebook Friend's birthday
    and don't I want to wish
    this Friend a Happy Birthday

My finger hurts from all the likes I press
    and too often write Happy Birthday as my
    Jewish guilt once again kicks in

Still, when I read someone lost someone close to them
    or is really sick, I stop to add a sad face
    and am sincere about it, often adding a brief
    comment (though I can't help wondering
    some if they're sure who I am)

And for the 30 Friends I actually know
    I'm sincerely happy for them when
    they post a publication or major award

Sometimes I feel a tinge of envy
    for some of my
    300 unknown Friends if they
    post some prestigious award
    that I was hoping for—but mostly not

Though I often sooth myself by falsely
    rationalizing and telling myself
    that maybe I was second in the contest
    or award I lost

Sometimes I stay away from Facebook for
    two days when I'm especially busy
    with deadlines or a family crisis

And those days when I don't have two hours
    to spend reading Facebook,
    I sometimes obsess about what I've missed

BRIDESMAID

I had only met her once at a family dinner
She was my fiancé's first cousin
My own bridesmaid a friend from
    first grade through our
    sophomore year at college
    had written me a formal third person note
    two weeks before my wedding and
    pulled out of it without any excuse
Earlier she had forced my college
    roommate out by the price of the
    bridesmaid's gown she was ordering
Though I begged my college roommate
    to just ignore the whole price issue
    and wear any pink
    cocktail dress she liked, my
    roommate refused and said she
    didn't want to ruin the wedding.

So Larry's cousin had her own
    bridesmaid's dress in pink tulle
    made in a week with so many crinolines under it,
    it looked as if an umbrella were open under her dress.

But she did look gorgeous and very sexy
    with her square cut low cut bodice
    as she walked down the aisle in front of me.
Actually, I thought she looked more glamorous than I did
    in my demure white silk understated
    low waisted Priscilla of Boston gown
    I had loved so much when I tried it on
    that I didn't try on any other gown.

But my bridegroom only saw me I know and anyway incest was not his th

The next year my bridesmaid
was getting married and had chosen
the same Manhattan hotel my in-laws
had chosen for me (after all, they wanted a lavish wedding for their son
and there was no way my widowed school teacher mother could afford
the Plaza that my in-laws wanted and insisted
on paying for).
I liked them a lot but realized that big events
were a necessary part of their lives.
(And I just wanted to get married.)
Their friends were still talking about my
groom's Bar Mitzvah almost ten years ago at the Waldorf Astoria.

My bridesmaid asked if she
could borrow my wedding gown.
Of course, I said yes in gratitude for her
being my bridesmaid at the last moment
and to also try to weave my
in-law's family even closer.

As she walked down the long
aisle in the same room wearing my
wedding gown from the year before,
I was startled to see her mother had
had a seamstress cover the entire gown
in sequins so it shimmered
and flashed and had lost its elegance
but gained a Las Vegas show girl look.
I had to admit she looked beautiful
but she probably would have in any gown.

When she returned my bridal gown torn and stained, I gave it away to charity.

MY NEW WEDDING RING

My husband gave it to me when
  we were married four years ago
It is actually three separate rings
  that fit tightly into each other
  the way pieces of a jig saw puzzle
  snap together
The ring in the middle is yellow gold
The two rings on either side white gold
  that have several really tiny diamonds
The ring says George Jensen under the band
The ring was made larger to fit over my arthritic
  knuckles
  I remember in high school
I had the second smallest size finger
  measured for our senior ring—size 4 1/2
Now I am a 9 with my swollen knuckles
  though the bottom of my finger is a 7
But the ring is beautiful
  even if my fingers aren't
  and I haven't worn a wedding band for 20 years
  since my 20-year marriage was over
When I look at it,
  it reminds me that it's
  never too late to find love
  whatever one's age
I give my single friends
  male and female hope they tell me
  though so many of them have told
  me they wouldn't be happy
  wearing my husband's dead third wife's
  wedding ring

I tell them I'm lucky I'm
  not superstitious

IT IS EASIER TO FALL IN LOVE WITH YOUR POEM THAN A MAN

Your poem doesn't tell you what to do
Your poem is an adventure you can control
Your poem doesn't object when you want to change something about it
Your poem will never leave you even if you don't look at it for years

Still, your poem cannot keep you warm in bed like a man

MY NEIGHBOR'S GARDEN

for Susie Choi

My neighbor who loves to garden
so much, she even pulls
the weeds from my tiny adjoining
backyard

She tells me she worries
about her plants
and loses sleep at night
thinking about the deer
eating the leaves and flowers
she's planted: blue hyacinths,
pale pink roses, peach trees,
pear trees and more whose Latin
names I don't remember

She has cleared the small wilderness
that first greeted her just as she
cleared space for herself when
she arrived from Korea decades ago
and raised three daughters virtually
on her own working so hard to give them
the promised *American Dream*

I remember the words she told me she told them
"I'll do my share and you do yours"
And they did: two daughters valedictorians
of a fine public school, one now a lawyer
and councilwoman
often visiting their mother with their children
Not so different from my neighbor
who diligently gardens when she is
not working and worries about her
plants at night

IDEAL DAY

My ideal day would be sitting at home
with a new Philip Roth novel
(probably impossible since he died
last year and gave up writing novels
several years before that)

My ideal day would be the phone ringing
and my younger son saying
he had finally gotten a job in his field
the travel industry (though like the
typewriter repair business, the travel
agent is on the job endangered list)

My ideal day would be the mail arriving with
a letter from my doctor saying all
my lab work was now normal

My ideal day would be having a number of
Kit Kat bars next to me as I read

My ideal day would be my grandchildren's mother saying
that since my son has a good job, she is thinking of
going back to him (maybe the most impossible thing
on my list)

My ideal day would be complete silence from our president—no tweets
or Instagrams, no press releases
as he sits in the Oval Office
watching game shows

My ideal day would be news reports without
one incident of racial violence,
prejudice against immigrants, gun violence,
bombing or children starving in Yemen,
Syria or our own country

But my ideal day is as impossible and elusive for me
as Philip Roth coming back from the dead
and sitting down at his computer and typing out a new novel

THE MOST BEAUTIFUL MAN I EVER SAW

The most beautiful man I ever saw
    was Robert Redford
It was in the mid-seventies and
    he was lounging against
    a column inside the entrance
    of Madison Square Garden
    where the Knicks were playing
    that night though I don't remember
    who they were playing

I didn't really like basketball but
    my husband did and had
    season tickets for this
    team that was a star team
    that year and it was not
    unusual to see Woody Allen
    and Diane Keaton sitting
    in the stands as well as
    other celebrities who were
    regulars that winning season
I was wearing my favorite slenderizing
    one piece navy knit with its belt
    at my hips and its bell bottom pants

I was walking between my husband and
    his best friend Marty also our internist, whose wife
    did not like basketball and
    fortunately found an excuse not to go

I noticed Robert Redford as we walked through,
    noticed how he was staring at me—
    how he slowly looked me up and down
    with his incredible sultry eyes

And I was thrilled to have him do this but
    knew enough not to say anything
    about it to my husband

But Marty said, "Larry, did you see the way
Robert Redford kept staring at L— ?"

My husband said he hadn't noticed

I wondered if Robert Redford did this often
to other women as they walked by

I wondered what would happen if
I walked away from my husband and Marty
and up to Robert Redford and said
"Want to go?"

But, of course, there was no way I would
ever have done this—and I had a practical side—
I had children at home
I had a decent husband—

And if I had followed my impulse and
walked up to Robert Redford—
the most beautiful man I had ever seen,
he probably would have started to run for the
door as fast as Walt Frazier would
later sprint down the basketball court

MY SON'S DAUGHTER PHONES

My son's older daughter calls
me from her boyfriend's
apartment in Boston where
she went just before the
pandemic shelter- in-place
It was a smart move (and
typical of her smart
actions—from a Harvard
full scholarship to working
at Google) since she can
as easily work from
his place as from her
mother's apartment in
New York City
I ask her how she is, about her
work, how she likes being
in Boston
She calls me once a month
for a long catch up call
She asks me how I am
I say considering everything,
I'm managing except for
not being able to sleep
more than three hours
at a time but one good
thing is since I've lost my appetite
I have lost a lot of weight
I try to avoid mentioning her
father
I try to talk about the virus and
getting food safely and my
husband's restlessness at
staying in so much
She says, "Why are we not talking
about my father since it's
now two months that he's
been missing"

I tell her I'm doing everything
I can with a police
detective still looking and
my other son on top of
things and calling the
rental car company to
see if the car has been
recovered
She tells me she thinks maybe
he parked the car in a
remote area and may
have died from carbon
monoxide poisoning
She says that we should call
the cell phone company
and have them trace the
location of his phone
No one has suggested those
two things before though
I think my son's paranoia
made him select an
untraceable phone
In the last year, she has
distanced herself from
me—something about
me has irritated her or
maybe I remind her of
her father's issues
But tonight she is concerned
about me—tells me
it will be bad for me
mentally if I just focus
on that
She tells me she loves me
She says I should be prepared
for the worst

SO MUCH TIME HAS GONE BY SINCE I'VE HEARD FROM HIM

I got an email from him today
So much time has gone by since I've heard from him
I dated him almost 40 years ago
I met him at a poetry reading
    at Saint Clements in Manhattan
I had just broken up with the worst guy
    I had ever lived with, a guy I had met
    when I was having a walking nervous breakdown
    after leaving my husband,
    a guy who played in a rock band
    (though they hardly had any gigs)
    a guy who smoked 18 joints at night,
    a guy with no job and didn't seem anxious
    to get one but content to live off me for now

The poet that night asked me if I'd like to go
    out for coffee and something to eat
I said, *"Yes"*
Still smarting from feeling used by
    my recent ex-boyfriend,
I uncharacteristically said to this poet
    as we were ordering
"If you want to be platonic friends,
    let's split the bill"
"But if you want us to be romantic,
    you pick up the check"
"I'll pick up the check," he said without hesitating

I thought he was smart—a PhD in Chemistry and
    a JD degree
He had been married and divorced twice
He was an editor of a poetry magazine
I was an editor of a poetry magazine
    although mine was a fledgling one
He liked my poetry
We started to date

He took me to an Art Deco Diner
and to a charming neighborhood
    restaurant near his Chelsea apartment
He had a bed on a platform
    with a ladder I'd climb up
He told me he had been with a lot of women
He told me I was the fifth best in bed
    which I took as a compliment
He gave me a great blurb
    for my first book
    except for the sting of calling me
    middle-aged (something I wouldn't
    mind someone calling me now)
He gave me a customized tape of
    his favorite rockabilly and country
    western songs which I loved
He said he'd marry me if I lost 15 pounds
I thought he was dating me exclusively as
    I was dating him
He told me he was dating another woman
    a woman he shared his
    interest in bird watching with
And he had told her he would marry
    her if she passed her bar exam this third try

He told me he was moving to a cold city in the
    Midwest for a great opportunity in a prestigious
    law firm

The other woman passed the bar exam
I never even tried to lose one pound
They married and moved to the Midwest
Somehow I didn't feel the least bit hurt
    and went on to the next poet
    who asked me out

MY TWO LIVES

This week I am definitely living two lives
At this moment I am leading a poetry
    workshop for mature adults by Zoom
It is a joyful time because the poets who
    joined today are as professional
    as many I've heard at Dodge Festivals
It makes me wonder how important
    it is to start early or at least
    start at an MFA years ago
    with colleagues, friends, and classmates
    who will be future networking editors
    of journals or even publishers—to form the
    Old Boys or even Old Girls Club
    where they reach out to
    help each other
Still, I tell myself that today it is
    often like a lottery—someone
    has to win one of those prestigious contests
    and get a book published through it
    and maybe win a sizeable chunk of money
But though the reality of it is hard,
    it is not impossible
And even if it doesn't work out with so many
    MFA students (some on a goal of 100 submissions
    and possibly 100 rejections)
    sending out poems
    is more like a factory making thousands
    of masks on a deadline for this pandemic
Still, for a really true poet (whatever that means)
    the jubilation from writing a poem
    he or she (or more politically correct today they) feel
    is the ultimate poetry happiness—
    greater than any contest
    or publication can ever bring

My second life can be categorized
    by my day today
By 10 o'clock with our rescue dog Toffee
    fed, walked and played with,
    I am waiting in the line at
    Morristown Hospital to be allowed
    to go upstairs after being checked
    that I don't have a fever
    or cough or haven't been to
    a list of states other than New Jersey lately
    I'm tagged and despite social
    distancing am on a packed elevator
    going up to the 5th floor
I am definitely concerned about getting Covid-19
I get my nerve up and politely
    ask another visitor
    if she can pull her mask over her nose
She says her asthma makes it
    difficult for her to breathe
    but pulls it up anyway
I say I understand and it's all
    so hard and thank her
I can't help but think how her
    saying "I can't breathe"
    has no political implications
    but how in this current time, it's
    almost impossible not to think of George Floyd
I wash my hands with the disinfectant
    foam on the wall
    and then again next
    to the entrance of my husband's room
He had a procedure (we used to call it operation)
    yesterday and has not
    had regular food for a week
I pull down my mask, kiss him hello
He smiles

I give him The New York Times
I tell him I have to leave in 45 minutes
    to lead my Zoom
    workshop at home but will
    come back to the hospital
    when it's over and stay with him
    until visitors have
    to leave at 8PM
I tell him he's looking better and am not
    certain that's true
    or just something
    I want to believe

Actually, I have a third life I'm leading
    that never seems to leave me—
    that constantly haunts me
My son is still missing and
    it's now more than four months

HOSPITAL BED

Each night I get into
my husband's hospital bed
I try to ignore the various tubes
infiltrating his long body
He has always liked to
sleep close to me
The bars of the bed jamb into
the eight inches allotted for me
"Move over," he says
"There's no room," I answer
But he is content, his arm around me
And I am comfortable even with iron
bars pressing into me
knowing he is content

UNCONDITIONAL LOVE

My grandchildren whom I rarely see
because of distance and some other things
despite their own busy lives and
mostly lack of interest in my life and activities
compared to their own activities
like papers due, cheerleading,
friends' activities, social life
are always polite
but somehow I feel they
are anxious to get
off the phone with me
as soon as possible
though they try to hide this
by often saying things like
"Do you want to speak to my father?"
or "I'm with my friends"
I am like their adult cheerleader
always praising them as bright,
exceptionally good looking,
having interesting ideas,
telling them how proud I am of them.
To me all of this is true though
I admit to being subjective
where they're concerned.
I think sometimes though
they seem to like my optimism about them,
they may also find this praise embarrassing.
No matter what to me questionable choices
they've made in school (and actually very few),
I take a positive slant.
I have never yelled at or criticized
any of my grandchildren
even when I was with them.
Of course, if it came to safety,
I might mildly say
something that I was concerned about

like their eating so little, or studying so hard
and not getting enough sleep or skydiving
(luckily only told after the fact)
but then I always put a positive slant on it
like their sense of conscientiousness,
or sense of adventure or
trying to look their best.
I tell them even if
I don't always like what they might be doing
in the future, I will always love them
and they can count on me to try to help them
and be on their side no matter what.
I think the one thing they know they have
and will always have from me is unconditional love.

They always end our brief phone calls, with
"I love you, Grandma" and even
sometimes "I miss you."
(Of course, I usually say it first.)
But still I try to believe them.

OBSESSION

My most recent obsession
is continually washing my hands
I have a supply of tiny hand sanitizers
in my bag
I have a large bottle I risked going into
Walgreens to get
when I kept calling early in
the pandemic to ask if they had gotten
any in and they replied yes
and they had just put it at the
front counter and it would be
gone soon
And so they couldn't hold it for me but
I'd better come in now
if I wanted it and, of course, only
one bottle per customer
I finally got a bottle from Facebook—
I think it came from China by
"slow boat from China"
It took months to get to my door step
and I have a bottle in my car,
in my kitchen, in my bathroom

But mostly, I am seriously obsessive when I visit my
husband each day at the hospital
where they have
foam disinfectant every few feet
on the walls

I wash my hands when I hand
him *The New York Times*
and *Star Ledger* from home
I wash my hands when I hand him
his cell phone to call his
daughter in California

I wash my hands after I touch
    my cell phone
I wash my hands after I pull
    up his thin blanket to
    keep him warm
    when I touch the bed rails,
    the tray, the box of tissues,
    and, of course, the elevator buttons

And I try not to use the bathrooms but sometimes
    if I've been visiting for ten hours,
    I use the bathroom,
    wash my hands after opening the door
    and for every single
    step in the process of bathroom
    routine in that enclosed space—
    even tinier than the elevator
    that seems to be crowded
    with masked heavy breathers

I know my constant hand washing is obsessive
    whether after bringing in a food package
    or the mail or delivered newspapers
    or even taking the parking ticket at the hospital garage
    and later pushing all the buttons
    to pay with my credit card

Still, the only time I don't wash my hands
    is when I lower my mask
    to kiss my husband
    hello or on my way out
    when I kiss him *goodbye*

I GUESS I'M GOING TO DIE SOON BUT I'M NOT HAPPY ABOUT IT

I guess I'm going to die soon
but I'm not happy about it
But I think some of my family
might be relieved to have the
burden of me and embarrassment
of me finally gone from our planet

As for my poetry colleagues,
they will moan and groan and
some will write competitive
memorial poems about me
and read those at the "celebration
of life" my closest "poet sister"
will have for me and, of course, get a lot
of publicity for herself (though her
grief will be genuine)

My family in D.C. who sees me once a year
for 90 minutes probably will feel guilty
(especially my wonderful son who
sacrificed spending time with me and
having his children spend time with me to help
his "Dennis the Menace" brother
with rent and food expenses to save me a free-lance poet
living on $885 monthly Social Security
the stress of keeping my son from a homeless existence)

And I realize that not seeing my older son and his children
is actually the way my son's beautiful wife
(who is an exceptionally good mother
and makes my son happy I know)
balances my son's actions since she understandably
resents all the money my son spends to help his brother survive

My sweet dog Nelly who has abandonment
issues will truly grieve for my absence
as will my relatively new handsome
husband though I am his fourth wife
and he has "rake" in his DNA and
I have asked him to wait eight minutes
at Shiva before he starts to flirt
with one of my female divorced or
widowed friends—

And he agrees

THE JUGGLER

Everyone I know
tries to juggle too many things
(as even you do as you read these poems possibly thinking
about your lawn that needs mowing)
A mother spooning out Cheerios for breakfast
but her thesis calling her from her dusty desk
Even our president juggling the emergency health issues
of our country with his own overinflated balloon ego tweets
I juggle my husband's needs for my undivided attention in bed
with my son's emergency that is unwanted
All this juggling we all do—
It's like trying to catch rain with your outstretched hands

WHENEVER I SEE A MAN

Whenever I see a man,
I wonder what he would
be like in bed
I've been doing this
since I was a young teen
(although it would be years
before I'd lose my virginity)
But I somehow never did this with
family members and immediately
negated any picture of my father,
brother or cousins in any
possible sexual encounter

And though I had no real knowledge but
had a feeling most of the
guys I met also did this to us females
or if gay to the same sex

I remember once a lover
(before I slept with him)
told me "You never really
know someone until
you've slept together."
At the time I wondered
if he were saying it just
to get me into bed
but he seemed to really
believe it himself and there
was no doubt in my mind
that you'd know a lot more
about the person if you
did have sex

Still, today decades later
and an official member
of AARP, and content

in my recent marriage
of four years with no desire
to ever sleep with any other
man but my new husband again

I still find myself when I see a new
man wondering what he'd be like in bed

AN IMMIGRANT MOTHER TALKS TO HERSELF AT THE MEXICAN BORDER DETENTION CENTER IN TORNILLO, TEXAS

And though I thought crossing the border
was saving my three year old son
from a future like his older fourteen year
old brother killed by M13 gang members for
resisting to join
And though I thought I'd save my five year old
daughter from the dangers of rape in puberty
like her cousin from those same
gang members
And though I imagined a life in a small Texas town with
a decent school system where they can dream of being
a teacher or even president (though I hope not like this
one who wants a wall and yesterday rips my children from me)
But tonight sleepless in this detention cell, I imagine the cries of my niños
not understanding why we are separated, the younger one missing
his pacifier (maybe just as much or more than me)
And I think our lives are a smashed piñata that is empty.

POEM WRITTEN A YEAR AGO

—for Gail (1939-2016)

My friend is going through Chemo
She tells me she has lost her hair
        and that is upsetting her more
        than the Chemo—that her
        wonderful daughter took her
        for a wig
No one can tell, I say
That's true, but I'll know
A couple of weeks earlier
        she had told me privately
        that the doctors said lymphoma
        and she was completely
        freaked out
Who wouldn't be, I say
        and then add the necessary
        They cure that a lot I think
        though I have virtually no medical
        knowledge about it

Today I am having a violent reaction
        to the antibiotics I'm on for
        a minor problem
I find myself terribly nauseous
        sitting on the bathroom tile
        and throwing up into the toilet
        the way I did the first three months
        of my pregnancy so many decades ago
I can't stand this, I think
        then think about my friend with
        a port now in her chest getting
        another round of Chemo
        and surgery scheduled for
        later this summer
My husband asks me how I feel
I think again of Gail and reply, *I'm fine*

ON HEARING OF JOHN ASHBERY'S DEATH

Years ago, when I was just starting my magazine,
John Ashbery was teaching at Brooklyn College
I was just an adjunct at FDU in New Jersey
and one of my colleagues was taking a poetry
workshop with Ashbery and suggested I go with
her to class. In those early years of my magazine,
I'd try to get work from established poets
by driving to their readings
and asking them for a poem for my poetry journal—
possibly a new piece they'd just read.

And though Brooklyn College was an even longer trip than usual,
I thought sitting in on Ashbery's workshop and the possibility
of publishing one of his poems worth the long trip.

I remember how awed the group seemed. I felt awed by his
presence though rather baffled by some of his poems
despite their luminous language.
When the workshop was over,
I offered to give him and some of his students a ride back to the City.
He accepted. I gave him a copy of my magazine and said I'd be honored
if he would consider sending a poem to it.

We piled into my car, Ashbery in the passenger seat,
a couple of his favorite students in the back.
It was raining hard. I could barely see and have several
good friends who refuse to drive with me
because of my style of driving.

Everyone in the car seemed to be clutching the seat
in front of them except John Ashbery
who had his hand braced on the glove compartment.
"Brake, Brake," he yelled as I barely missed a turn onto 8th Avenue.
When he finally got out at his white brick Chelsea apartment house
along with his students,
he barely mumbled a goodbye.
I never did get a poem from him.

ODE TO A PATERSON TEACHER

Years ago I walked into a public school class
in Paterson, NJ as a visiting poet—
something I still sometimes do today
This now gritty city somehow retained its patina
of Hamilton's vision and W C Williams' beauty,
the Great Falls nearby cascading with an iridescent force—
But here in this classroom where students in neat uniforms
of blue button down shirts and freshly pressed khakis,
diversity of mahogany or caramel faces stating
African or Caribbean heritage with a very few pale faces
of new immigrants from Serbia or Croatia—

This energetic but empathetic teacher puts her arm around
a sweet faced eighth grade student and asks me if I noticed
his writing and alertness during class—
I admit I had—
She tells me she's trying to get this brilliant foster child a scholarship
to a private boarding school where his exceptional
intellectual gifts can blossom—
"And if that doesn't work," she continues, "I plan
to adopt him myself"
She is serious and determined and
I cannot help but wonder how much better
our world would be if her caring and kindness were
infectious and something all teachers could
catch before they stepped into their first classroom

A POLICE CAR ACROSS THE STREET FROM THE SYNAGOGUE ON ROSH HASHANAH

Years ago as a teenager I walked to
synagogue on Rosh Hashanah
my only worry that my new holiday
dress would not make me look thinner
my only worry that the boy I liked
would not smile at me
Feeling as safe walking with my
parents as I would ever feel

Today decades later with my new
husband (though neither of us is statistically new),
I'm startled to see
a police car with officers directly
across the street from the
synagogue this High Holiday as
well as another police officer guarding
the entrance, his eyes scanning
everyone on this street,
his hand above his holster

And I think how the presence of
police outside the
synagogue today is as disturbing
as a Rosh Hashanah dinner
with a pitcher of milk and plate of
brisket next to it on the holiday table

A GOOD MORNING BLUE SKY

I walk outside
to a Good Morning Blue Sky
No 1010 news
replete with traffic jams
on Rt 3 East (always Rt 3)
My sweet dog walking
without her leash at my
ankles, the cherry blossoms bursting
forth this third week in April,
this birthday week for my husband, me (and even our dog)
and I imagine my mother out in this glorious
scenario more than half a century ago
pushing my pram through Branch Brook Park
under a canopy of cherry blossoms probably
feeling the sun on her raised face—finally with a flat belly again
though her breasts are larger and throbbing with milk
She is so relieved to be alive (after the unexpected
ordeal of labor pain that no one prepared her for)
Perhaps she dreams of my future still in front of her
a shimmering sunny cascade of cherry blossoms

And a few miles away, a few years earlier,
in April, my husband's mother
smiles and wonders about
the mystery of his life as she
wheels his carriage toward his future

I'VE ALWAYS WORRIED

I've always worried
I think it's in my DNA
At seven, I worried I'd die
when the ether rubber mask
was put over my face

At twelve, I worried for a year
that my mother (whom
everyone said I didn't look
at all like) wasn't my
real mother when her
sister told me my mother
was my father's second
wife and swore me to secrecy
or my mother would never
forgive her for telling me

At sixteen, I worried my father
would die of pancreatic cancer
He did

At twenty, I worried my fiancé
would die in a car crash
before our wedding

At twenty-one, I worried I'd die
in childbirth
It was close, but I didn't

At thirty, I worried my son
would drown at overnight camp
even though I'd asked the camp owner
if any child had ever died at his camp
before my son was signed up
and the owner answered "No"

But I never worried a tree would fall
on my neighbor and kill her
though she managed to push
her son out of its path

And I never worried that
there would be a terrorist attack
that would bring down the
World Trade Towers with so many
killed, including my friend's son and my
first grade granddaughter's seat mate's father

And I never worried that you
wouldn't love me and so far
I still don't worry about that

THE LAST TIME

The last time I saw my younger son
  was after I rented a Hertz car
  for him near Paramus, filled the gas tank,
  went to an ATM to give him some extra money
  he needed and watched him zoom down the road
I drove to a nearby 7/11 to get a cup of coffee since
  I hadn't had time for breakfast because of my
  early school workshop in Paterson
My son was in the 7/11 holding a large cup of Pepsi
  and an Entenmann's Peanut Butter Tandy cake
He beamed when he saw me, and tried to hug me
  as he put down his cup of Pepsi on the counter
  where it immediately spilled covering candy, paper items, little
  flashlights and some other things (he gets that clumsiness from
  me who is always dropping things)
The clerk, probably the owner, scowled at my son
"Oh, I'm sorry, I'm sorry," my son said and there was no doubt he meant it
That was the last time four months ago that I saw my son
  though I have reported him as a missing person
  though he didn't call me on Mother's Day—first time ever
  didn't call me on my my birthday—first time ever
  didn't call his ex-wife on her birthday—first time ever
  didn't call his daughter on her birthday—first time ever
The Hertz car has disappeared though reported missing to the police—
The police detective has not been able to find him
The missing report is in
The morgues have been checked

"Where do you think he is ?" I ask my husband, his stepfather
"Dead and in the trunk of the rental car," he replies

AS WINTER SETS IN

As winter sets in, I wonder if I'll survive it
My husband died two weeks ago—
Of course, I miss him and it's odd
  to be in this house without his strong
  presence but the dog is here and
  misses him too as Toffee sleeps where my husband
  slept near the bottom of the bed
  where Jim's feet would have been
My younger son is also dead after
  being missing for 4 1/2 months with the anxiety
  of wondering if he had been tortured, murdered,
  locked in the trunk of the rental car that had been then
  thrown in the river
No matter how much I continue my work commitments
  during the day, that sad ache returns like panic
  intermittently throughout the day—
I don't think I'll ever get over the sadness
  of my younger son's death
  and several of my poet friends who have
  also lost a child tell me I won't get over it but
  I'll get through it
And I know there's nothing I can change so I go on—
  not one day at a time but one hour at a time
And, yes, the writing helps—maybe the only thing
  that helps except for my older son's caring phone
  calls each day

But now with Jim gone, I wonder if I'll survive this winter
  since I naturally focused on Jim's illness and because
  of Covid skipped my own medical appointments
And now I am faced with bleak news from my own doctors
  after finally going in for tests
And I can't help but wonder as winter sets in
  if I'll ever survive it

CPSIA information can be obtained
at www.ICGtesting.com
Printed in the USA
LVHW111312040621
689372LV00001B/4